Cowboy Crock Pot Cooking

Real Old West Cowboy Chow Easily Cooked in Your Crock Pot

Brent Younger

Cowboy Crock Pot Cooking: Real Old West Cowboy Chow Easily Cooked in Your Crock Pot, Copyright © 2013 by Mix 'n Sip, LLC

ISBN 978-1-939860-90-3

Published by Mix Books, LLC
mix-booksonline.com

Table of Contents

DEDICATION

To the cowboys of old, who spent up to four straight months in the saddle, eating every meal at the chuck wagon. To the pioneers who tamed the land and the saloons and ranches where they gathered and ate and drank together. And to modern day cowboys who want a little taste of the Wild West.

This image, entitled "The Cow Boy", taken by John C. H. Grabill (1866–1934) in 1887 is in the Public Domain and is available from the United States Library of Congress's Prints and Photographs division under the digital ID ppmsc.02638.

INTRODUCTION

I don't pretend to be an expert on cowboy lore or cowboy cooking, but I do love hearty foods and there's never been a John Wayne movie I didn't like. In fact, in a past life, I'm pretty sure I must have been a ranch hand, or maybe something more like a gun-toting desperado.

At any rate, I do know how to cook and I do know how to read and along the way I've indulged my cowboy fantasies by delving into some of the old recipes that I've come across from the late 1800s and early 1900s and updating them for today's kitchen (and I've thrown in a few newer ones too). Some of these recipes would have been rustled up by "Cookie" on cattle drives and a lot of them were regular fare on the ranch.

Texas rancher, Charles Goodnight, is credited with the invention of the chuck wagon, a kind of kitchen on wheels in 1866. He purchased an old Studebaker (yep, they've been around a long time) army wagon and outfitted it with shelves and boxes for supplies and cooking utensils and a pull-down work-table at the back.

Before the chuck wagon, cow hands pretty much had to eat dried beef and biscuits that they supplied and carried in their packs, or whatever they could catch and kill, so they were often hungry. Goodnight was a pretty smart guy. He realized a cowboy would work much harder on a full stomach, so he hired a cook, stocked up the chuck wagon and made sure there was always a hearty meal at the end of the day.

We're all familiar with scenes of a big pot over a camp fire, filled with beans or stew that Cookie had prepared. And at home, whether you were cooking over an open fire or had the newest range to feed 20 ranch hands, the stew pot was one of the most important items in the kitchen. Nowadays, we have the crock pot.

Coffee, cornbread, onions, potatoes, molasses, lard and beef were staples and meats were often salted to preserve them. Beans were also staples but, on the trail, they were not cooked as often as you might think because they took too long.

The cowboy diet was a wholesome diet. People worked long and hard; no-one cared about calories or low fat, so don't expect to see that here. Meats would have been tougher than we're used to – animals weren't pumped up with hormones and fed stuff they were never meant to eat – and slow cooking would have been the best way to make a meal tender. That said, cooking in a crock pot today is a good way to save some money because you can use cheaper cuts of meat and still enjoy a really delicious and hearty meal.

Most of the ingredients you'll be really familiar with, except maybe lard. Lard gets a bad rap. I grew up eating the flakiest pastry and the crunchiest fried chicken cooked with lard. Just make sure you get the non-hydrogenated kind – that's the genuine stuff.

~ Brent Younger

Take note: Please keep in mind that measurements given here are all for USA, so those of you in other countries may need to make some adjustments.

COWBOY CROCK POT COOKING: BEEF

Git Along Beef Pot Roast

This is based on a recipe served in a hotel in Colorado back in the late 1800s. Make this a more complete meal by adding peeled and cubed potatoes to the crock pot. Serve it with some fresh-baked Hot Rocks (biscuits).

- 4 lb chuck roast
- 3 tbs olive oil or lard
- 1 cup beef stock
- 4 tbsp ketchup
- 1 tbsp Worcestershire sauce
- 1 (1 oz) package of dry onion soup mix
- ½ clove minced garlic
- 2 tsp salt
- 1 tsp celery seed
- ½ tsp black pepper
- ½ lb sliced white mushrooms

1. Use the oil to sear the roast on all sides in a saute pan, then set it aside

2. Pour off the excess oil and add the stock to the pan, bringing to a simmer while scraping the bottom then pour it in the crock pot
3. Add all other ingredients except the mushrooms and stir
4. Now add the mushrooms and the roast, making sure to coat the beef with the liquid
5. Cover and cook on low setting for 8 to 10 hours

Oriental Saloon Stew

The Oriental Saloon opened in 1880 in Tombstone, AZ. It was described as "the most elegantly furnished saloon this side of the Golden Gate" and was a favored hangout for cowboys and bad boys. Even Wyatt Earp had a share in the business, which was a good thing as the place was notorious for shootings. This recipe is as close as it gets to the real thing.

- 2 1/2 lbs beef, cut in cubes

- 2 tablespoons flour
- 1 tablespoon paprika
- 1 teaspoon chili powder plus 3 tablespoons chili powder
- 2 teaspoon salt
- 3 tablespoons lard or oil
- 2 onions, sliced
- 1 clove garlic, minced
- 1 28 oz can tomatoes
- 1 tablespoon cinnamon powder
- 1 teaspoon ground cloves
- 1/2 - 1 teaspoon crushed red peppers
- water
- 2 cups chopped potatoes
- 2 cups chopped carrots

1. Mix the flour, paprika, chili powder and salt and coat the beef
2. Brown the coated beef in hot oil for just a few minutes
3. Add onions and garlic, and cook until soft
4. Move the beef mix to your crock pot
5. Add water to the pan and bring to a simmer while scraping the browned bits off the bottom, then add to the crock pot
6. Combine all the remaining ingredients in the crock
7. Cover and cook on low setting for about 8 hours

Cheese Burger Pie

Bisquick has been around since the 1930s. I don't know when this recipe was first created but it sure is good.

- 2 ½ lbs hamburger
- 2 onions, chopped
- 2 cups grated cheddar cheese
- 1 cup Bisquick mix
- 1 ¾ cups milk
- 3 eggs
- salt to taste

1. Brown the ground beef and drain most of the fat before adding to the crock pot with the chopped onions
2. Sprinkle the cheese on top of the beef and onion mix
3. In a separate bowl, mix Bisquick, eggs and milk 'til smooth
4. Pour Bisquick mix over the top but do not stir
5. Cover and cook on low for 7 to 8 hours

Yee Haw Beef and Cabbage

Instead of first stuffing the cabbage, we're putting everything in the crock and adding the cabbage last.

- 1 ½ lbs lean ground beef
- ½ tsp pepper
- 1/3 cup uncooked white rice
- 1 can condensed tomato soup
- 1 ½ teaspoon salt
- 1/4 teaspoon pepper
- 2 tablespoons butter
- 1 large onion, chopped
- 1 cup chopped celery
- 1 ½ cup hot water or beef bouillon
- 2 tablespoon cider vinegar or lemon juice
- 2 tsp fresh minced parsley
- 1 small head cabbage, quartered and stem removed

1. Combine condensed soup with water or bouillon
2. Add the soup mix with all other ingredients except cabbage to the crock pot
3. Cover and cook on low for 6 to 8 hours
4. At least an hour before serving, lay the cabbage quarters on top. Add a little extra water if the meat mix seems too dry. Continue cooking on low

5. After 1 hour, check the cabbage is cooked. If it's not quite done, turn the heat to high and leave for an additional 15 to 20 minutes.

6. To serve, plate the cabbage first, then pour the meat over it.

Come and Get it Coffee Roast

Cowboys loved their coffee. Here's a recipe where coffee is actually used in cooking a roast. You'll need to start prepping it a couple of days ahead but don't worry, it's dead easy.

- 3 – 5 lb beef brisket
- 1 dozen garlic cloves, halved
- 1 onion, chopped
- 1 cup of apple cider vinegar (raw vinegar is best)
- 2 cups strong brewed coffee
- 2 cups water

1. Cut slits in the brisket and insert the garlic into the slits
2. Pour the vinegar over the meat and work it into the slits
3. Marinate for 24 to 48 hours, refrigerated, of course, and basting occasionally
4. Place in the crock pot with the onion
5. Combine the coffee and water and pour over the meat
6. Cover and cook on low for 8 – 10 hours

If you think a Coffee Boiler was something to make your brew in, well, you'd be wrong. It was another name for a lazy, no-good… you get the picture. Someone who'd be more 'n likely to sit around the campfire with the coffee pot than lend a hand.

California Boiled Beef

In late 1800s San Francisco, when drovers arrived after herding cattle for months and eating beans and mouse pie while on the trail, a savory plate of tender boiled beef was a favorite.

You'll start this recipe by making beef stock. I like to start the stock in the evening and let it simmer overnight. In the morning, all I have to do is drop in the brisket. It's quite a simple recipe and that slow cooking makes it really worthwhile.

- 3 lb beef brisket
- At least 1 lb beef bones
- ½ lb carrots, diced
- 2 turnips, diced
- 4 or 5 celery stalks, sliced
- 1 tsp dried thyme
- 3 bay leaves
- 15 peppercorns
- Salt to taste

1. To make the stock, add everything except the brisket to the crock pot
2. Add enough water to cover all the ingredients
3. Turn the crock pot on low and leave for 10 hours
4. At this stage you can remove the bones and discard them

5. Put the brisket in the pot, check your stock in case you need to add more seasoning
6. Continue to simmer on low for another five hours

Critter Meatloaf

According to the Oxford Companion to Food, meatloaf was first mentioned in print in the U.S. in 1899. It was no accident this this was immediately after the invention of the mechanical meat grinder by German inventor Karl Drais.

These days we think of critter as a general term for almost any animal but to a cow poke years ago, a critter was a cow.

- 2 lbs ground beef (even better – a mix of beef and bison)
- 6 slices white bread (stale is fine)
- 2/3 cup milk (aka cow juice)
- 3 eggs, beaten
- Salt and pepper
- ½ cup ketchup
- 2 tbsp brown sugar
- 1 tsp powdered mustard

1. Soak the bread in the milk then break it up and add to the meat, eggs and seasoning
2. Make sure your hands are clean then dig in and mix everything together
3. Form the mix into a round (or oval) to fit your crock pot and lay the meatloaf in
4. Mix together the ketchup, sugar and mustard and spread over the top of the meatloaf

5. Cover and cook on low for 7 – 8 hours (longer is OK)

6. Serve with mashed potatoes mixed with grilled onion and real bacon pieces

Oxtail Soup

Cowboy etiquette: "Don't take the last serving unless you're sure you're the last man." That's kind of hard to do, 'cause this soup really is mighty tasty.

- 2 lbs oxtails
- 3 oz butter
- 3 tbsp plain flour
- 2 1/2 quarts water or beef broth*
- 6 peppercorns
- 2 bay leaves
- 1 medium onion, chopped
- Salt to taste
- 2 medium potatoes, cut into cubes
- 3 carrots or 1/2 lb baby carrots, sliced
- 1 (16 ounce) can diced tomatoes

1. Coat the oxtails lightly in flour and saute in the butter to brown
2. Combine the oxtails in the crock with all the other ingredients
3. Cover and cook on low for 8 hours
4. Take out the oxtails and remove the meat from the bone
5. Put the meat back in the soup and cook for another 15 minutes

Pot Rustler's Stew

Here's a quick modern day meal for when you want to rustle up something delicious that's also easy to prepare. Pot Rustler was another name sometimes given to the cook.

- 1 pound ground beef
- 1 medium onion, coarsely chopped
- 1 box Betty Crocker* Bacon & Cheddar Scalloped Potatoes (5.1 oz)
- 1 can whole kernel corn, undrained
- 1 can cream of celery soup
- 1 cup milk
- Salt and pepper, to taste
- 2 tablespoons ketchup
- 1 tablespoon mustard
- 4 thick slices American cheese

1. In a skillet, brown the ground beef with the onions; drain off the fat when done
2. Place the bacon & cheddar potatoes, with the included seasoning mix, in the crock pot; top with milk, undrained corn and cream of celery soup
3. Top the potato mixture with ground beef and onions; salt and pepper to taste. Dot evenly with ketchup and mustard; top with cheese slices
4. Cover and cook on low for 7 to 9 hours

There's no real Betty Crocker, but the brand has been around since the late 1800s.

COWBOY CROCK POT COOKING: CHICKEN

Ranch Hand Chicken and Cheesy Dumplings

This is adapted from a recipe from a Nebraska ranch in the early 1900s. I've increased the amount of butter or lard used in the dumplings and reduced the milk to make a drier dumpling, which I find preferable, and replaced water with chicken stock.

This is a perfect workday meal. Just throw all the fixin's in the crock in the morning, take 10 minutes to prepare the dumplings (or make them the evening before) and leave them in the fridge to add to the stew when you get home.

For the stew:
- 4 to 6 lb chicken, cut into pieces
- 4 cups of chicken broth
- 2 stalks of celery, chopped
- 2 lg carrots, chopped
- 1 lg onion, chopped
- 1 tbsp of your favorite seasoning blend (I use Mrs. Dash garlic and herbs)
- A few peppercorns (or ground black pepper)

For 6 or 7 dumplings (they will almost double in size as they cook):

- 1 cup plain flour
- 2 tsp baking powder
- pinch of salt
- 4 tbsp cold butter or lard
- ¼ - cup cold milk

- ½ tsp dried sage
- ½ tsp dried parsley
- 1 ½ oz grated cheddar cheese (those of you dieting can leave this out, but ya'll will be missing one of the best things)

1. Clean the chicken and cut into pieces
2. To the crock pot, add the chicken, broth, celery, carrot, onion, seasoning and peppercorns
3. Turn on low and leave for about 8 hours
4. In a separate bowl, combine the flour, baking powder, sage and parsley
5. Cut in cold butter with a pastry cutter or use your fingers to rub the butter into the flour
6. If you're using the cheese, now is the time to mix it in
7. Add the milk and mix with your hands to make a moist dough (you may need to add just a little more milk)
8. Break the dough into golf ball size rounds and set on a plate. Cover loosely with plastic wrap and refrigerate

9. 30 minutes before you're ready to eat, plop the dumplings into the simmering stew and push them just below the juices. Re-place the lid

Easy Cowboy Slow Chicken

Here's something from the modern day cowhand.

- 4-6 chicken breasts
- 2 tablespoons brown sugar
- 1 tablespoons Dijon Mustard
- 2 cups salsa (any type)
- 1 (15 ounce) can corn, drained
- 1 (15 ounce) can black beans, drained and rinsed
- ½ cup sour cream (optional)
- Brown rice (for serving)

1. Place chicken in a 5-6 quart greased slow cooker
2. In medium bowl mix brown sugar, mustard, and salsa
3. Pour mixture over chicken. Add water to cover chicken, if needed. Cook on low for 6-8 hours or high for 4 hours

4. With 30 minutes of cook time remaining remove the lid and shred the chicken using two forks

5. Add beans, corn, and sour cream to the slow cooker and mix with the chicken. Replace lid and cook for remaining 30 minutes

6. Serve over rice with sour cream

German Chicken Stew

From the Jewish Cookery Book, 1871, this recipe would have been more common back east. However, there were many adventurous Jews who sought their fortunes along the ever-shifting frontier of the American West and who would have appreciated the stew.

This is pretty much the original recipe, though I've gauged the measurements to my taste. The only tricky part was 'sweet herbs,' which would have been a mix of things like sweet marjoram and summer savory, tied in a muslin bag. I've substituted thyme as the closest and most readily available herb. But you go right on ahead and change things to suit yourself if you want to.

- 4 lb – 5 lb chicken, cut up in small pieces
- 1 dozen peppercorns, cracked
- 1 tsp dried ginger
- ¼ cup chopped fresh parsley or 1 tsp dried parsley
- 1 tsp dried thyme
- 2 cloves minced garlic
- Salt to taste
- Lemon and parsley for garnish

1. Put all the ingredients except the garnish in your crock pot and just cover with water
2. Cook on low for 6 – 8 hours

3. According to Ester Levy, the author of the Jewish Cookery Book, this should be served with boiled carrots

Caballero Chicken Chili

If you've watched a lot of old cowboy movies like me, you'll know the word caballero gets bandied around a fair piece, and you're prob'ly thinkin' it refers to a Spanish cowhand. Well, you'd be wrong. El Caballero was a nobleman, skilled in horsemanship; it's only in American slang (and movies) that it got misused.

All that aside, this spicy dish will sure spin your spurs.

- 2 lbs chicken breast, cubed
- 1 onion, chopped
- 1 green bell pepper, chopped
- 2 jalapeno peppers, chopped (optional depending on how hot you can take it)
- 2 cans pinto beans
- 2 packages chili seasoning

- 2 cans Mexican style diced tomatoes

1. Put everything in the crock pot and give it a good stir
2. Cover and cook on low. It will be done in 4 to 5 hours but you can leave it longer if you add a little water

Cowboy wisdom: Don't squat with your spurs on.

Quick and Easy Cowpoke Chicken

In cowboy speak, a chickabiddy is a young chicken. It's also a term of endearment for children. So now you can feed chickabiddy to your chickabiddies. *That sounds kinda weird, doesn't it?*

- Chicken Breast halves, no skin
- 2 cups of your favorite Salsa (mild, medium, or hot)
- 1 tbsp Brown Sugar
- 1 tbsp Brown Mustard

1. Place chicken in crock pot
2. Mix all other ingredients in bowl and pour over chicken
3. Cook in crock pot on low for about 6 hours
4. Serve over rice

If you see a recipe for Chuck Wagon Chicken you'd likely think it's something with a bird. Well, it ain't. At least not to an old cowboy. He'd be expecting fried bacon. And Fried Chicken would be bacon that's been dredged in flour and then fried.

And I guess you all know a cowpoke is a cowhand. But it was also a device used around the neck of livestock to prevent them from breaking through the fencing. It would poke the beast when it came in contact with the fence.

Chicken and Wine

In the 1800s many ethnic family farms in Texas and the West harvested grapes and made wine that they then sold to saloons. So I figured I should include at least one recipe to celebrate Wild West wine country.

- 6 Chicken breasts (skinned & deboned)
- 1 or 2 tbsp olive oil
- 1 large onion (chopped)
- 16 oz can condensed mushroom soup
- 6 oz chicken broth
- 8 oz diced green olives
- 1 cup white wine

1. Cut chicken into cubes and brown lightly in the oil
2. Move the chicken to the crock and combine with all the other ingredients
3. Cook on high for 3 to 3½ hours or low for 6 to 8 hours
4. This is perfect served over egg noodles

COWBOY CROCK POT COOKING: PORK AND HAM

BBQ Ribs

These ribs will fall off the bone. You'll probably need only half the sauce, so keep the rest in the refrigerator; it won't be long before you're making these again. And by the way, it's okay to eat with your fingers. The food is clean. (That's cowboy etiquette)

- 3 lbs pork spare ribs
- 1 onion, diced
- For sauce:
- 1 cup ketchup
- 1 cup chili sauce
- ¼ cup cider vinegar
- ¼ cup steak sauce
- ¼ cup molasses
- 3 tbsp dry mustard
- 2 tbsp prepared horseradish
- 1 tbsp Worcestershire sauce
- 1 tbsp tabasco sauce
- 1 tbsp minced garlic

1. Make the sauce ahead of time by combining all the ingredients and whisking them together. Keep refrigerated until you're ready to use it.
2. Put the onion in the bottom of your crock pot
3. Lay the ribs on top and cover in sauce
4. Cover and cook on low for 8 – 10 hours

Ham and Pease Pudding

Those of you who have heard of pease pudding, made from dried split yellow peas, may know it by the name of pease porridge. It was one of U.S. President Andrew Jackson's favorite dishes, seasoned with onions, cloves, carrots, celery, butter, nutmeg, sour cream, salt, pepper, and sugar.

Traditionally, the pudding is cooked to a paste consistency and then allowed to cool. It is later cut up and eaten cold, often in a sandwich with the ham. However, I prefer to eat it as a hot accompaniment to a ham dinner.

- 1 ham hock
- 1 lb dried yellow split peas, soaked for at least 8 hours then washed and drained
- 12 cloves
- 1 cup grated carrot
- 1 whole onion, peeled
- 2 garlic cloves, minced
- Ground white pepper

1. Cut slits in the ham and tuck a clove into each one
2. To your crock pot add the ham hock, peas, carrot, onion and garlic. Pour in water until the hock is just slightly covered
3. Cover and cook on low for 8 hours. Check the pot occasionally to stir the pease mix and add more

water if it is getting too dry. The pudding should remain the consistency of grits

Appetite Pleasin' Pork Casserole

On the trail the 'cookie' might also be called gut robber, grub slinger, greasy belly, biscuit shooter, coosie, dough wrangler or dough belly. For all that, he got a lot of respect and had a lot of authority. After all, he was providing one of the most important things a cowboy needed – food.

- 1 ½ lbs cut up lean pork
- ¼ cup white flour
- 2 tbsp lard or olive oil
- 1 lb chopped potato
- ½ cup chopped celery

- ½ lb carrots
- ½ tsp thyme
- 1 pint chicken broth

1. Toss the pork pieces in the flour and brown in the lard
2. Add to the crock pot and combine with all the other ingredients
3. Cover and cook on low for 8 hours
4. Serve over fresh baked biscuits

Last Stand Stew

It's said this was a favorite of old General George Custer. His 'last stand' was June 25, 1876 in Montana.

- 3 lbs pork, cubed (or you could use beef)
- 3 tbsp lard or oil
- 1 onion, chopped
- 1 clove garlic, minced
- 2 med. carrots, chopped
- 2 sm. parsnips, chopped
- 2 celery stalks, chopped
- 1 green pepper, chopped
- 2 pints chicken stock
- 3 tbsp sweet paprika
- 1 tsp dry mustard
- 1 lb mushrooms
- 3 potatoes, peeled and diced
- 3 tomatoes, peeled and chopped

1. Heat the oil or lard in a fry pan and cook the onions 'til soft
2. Sprinkle the paprika over the onions and stir
3. Add the meat and cook until it is just seared
4. Transfer the meat mixture with all the other ingredients to your crock pot and stir
5. Cover and cook on high for 4 – 5 hours, or on low for 8 hours

Pork Pot Roast and Turnips

Cowboy wisdom: Don't name a pig you plan to eat.

- 4 lb pork shoulder roast
- 1 lg onion, sliced
- 2 lbs turnips, sliced
- 2 tsps dried thyme
- 2 cups chicken stock
- 2 tsps salt
- 1 tsp ground pepper
- 2 tbsp oil

1. Rub the salt and pepper over the roast
2. Heat the oil in a skillet and sear the meat (about 3 minutes on each side)
3. Move the roast to the crock pot
4. Add the onion and thyme to the skillet; saute until the onion is just beginning to turn brown
5. Add half the chicken stock to the pan and bring to a simmer. Stir and scrape the bottom of the pan to loosen any browned pork
6. Place the turnips around the roast in the crock and pour the mixture from the pan with the other cup of chicken stock over the meat and turnips
7. Cover the crock pot and cook on low for 8-10 hours, or high for 4 to 5 hours

Pork and Sauerkraut

The Pennsylvania Dutch likely brought this dish to the West. Traditionally, it was served on New Year's Day, to bring good luck.

By the way, the man who created the cowboy hat as we know it today was a Pennsylvanian. His name was John B. Stetson.

And here's another nugget for you. Tom Mix, a famous cowboy and actor from Pennsylvania, helped John Wayne get his start in the movies, handling props in the back lot of Fox Studios. Thought you might like to know that.

- 3 – 4 lb pork loin
- 1 lg green apple, peeled and shopped small
- 2 lbs sauerkraut (undrained)
- Salt and pepper

1. Set the pork in the crock pot
2. Sprinkle salt and pepper over it
3. Top with the apple then the sauerkraut
4. Cover and cook on low for 8 hours

COWBOY CROCK POT COOKING: BEANS

Blazing Saddle Sausage & Beans

Cowboy wisdom: A week spent around the campfire will tell you more about a man than living next to him for 10 years.

- 4 cups dried pinto beans
- 24 oz crushed tomatoes
- 1 lb pork sausages in the skin
- 2 jalapenos, chopped small
- 1 sweet onion, chopped
- Salt, pepper and garlic powder to taste

1. A day ahead, cover the beans in water and set aside to soak (at least 12 hours)
2. Drain the beans and put them in the crock pot
3. Add the other ingredients
4. Cover and cook on high for 4 – 5 hours, or on low for 6 – 8 hours

Did you know? Sausages were sometimes referred to as "mysteries," 'cause folk didn't know what they were made of.
A cowboy might call his beans Whistle Berries. No imagination needed to figure that one out.

Bodacious Baked Beans

From an early 1900s recipe. Salt pork these days is made from pork bellies, like bacon. It's not smoked or cured, though, and has a lot more fat but it's the fat and saltiness that make it such a good base ingredient for many dishes.

- 1 lb dried navy beans
- ¼ lb salt pork, diced
- 1 cup chopped onion
- 1 cup tomato sauce
- ¼ cup cider vinegar
- ½ cup molasses
- 1 tbsp dry mustard
- 1 tsp salt
- 1 tsp black pepper
- 1 tbsp Worcestershire sauce

1. Soak beans in water overnight
2. Drain and rinse the beans
3. Brown the salt pork in a skillet
4. When done, remove the salt pork and lightly saute the onions
5. Put the beans, salt pork, onions and all other ingredients in the crock
6. Cover and cook on low for about 8 hours. Stir occasionally and add a little water if the beans begin to dry

Old Fart Baked Beans

These beans will sure get you moving, and they're made simple by the use of 'airtights.' That's a term that was used for canned goods.

Canned beans were among the first convenience foods and were even in supply during the American Civil War in the 1860s.

- 1 lg. can baked beans
- 1 can lima beans, drained
- 1 can kidney beans
- 1 can chili beans

- 1 can butter beans, drained
- 1/2 to 1 lb. bacon, cut up
- 1 c. ketchup
- 3/4 c. molasses
- 3/4 c. brown sugar
- 1/2 onion, chopped
- ½ cup celery, chopped
- ½ cup chopped green bell pepper

1. Fry bacon crisp
2. Add onion, celery and green pepper and saute lightly
3. Combine onion mix, bacon and all the other ingredients in the crock pot
4. Cover and cook on low for 2 hours. For later eating, turn to 'warm' setting to keep beans hot
5. Do not let dry out. Add a little water if necessary

Coffee Beans

If you want a second helping of these, just yell, "Man at the Pot!" That's how a cowboy would ask someone to bring him another cup of coffee.

- 1 pkg. (1 lb.) pinto beans
- 1/2 lb. bacon, diced
- 1 lg. onion, chopped
- 2 cloves garlic, minced
- 3 c. six-shooter skink (cowboy speak for strong coffee)
- 1/2 c. molasses
- 2 tbsp. ketchup
- 1 tsp. dry mustard
- Salt & pepper to taste

1. Soak beans in water overnight; drain.
2. Saute the bacon
3. Add onion and garlic; saute until slightly translucent
4. Add the beans, bacon, onion and garlic to the crock and stir in coffee, molasses, ketchup, dry mustard, salt and pepper
5. Cover and cook on low for 6 – 8 hours

Hop Juice (Beer) Beans

After you eat a mess of these you'll be "stacked to a fill." That's cowboy speak for 'stuffed.'

- 1 lb. dry pinto beans, rinsed and checked for stones
- About 8 cups water
- 1 (12 oz.) can beer
- 1 lb. smoked ham hocks
- 1/2 cup chopped onion
- 1 (16 oz.) can tomatoes, cut up
- 2 tbsp. molasses
- 1 tsp. dry mustard
- 1/4 tsp. pepper
- 1/2 tsp. cumin
- Salt to taste

1. Rinse beans and combine with enough water to cover. Let soak overnight
2. Drain the beans and combine with all the other ingredients, plus 2 cups of water, in the crock pot
3. Cover and cook on low for 8 hours
4. When beans are ready, take out the ham hocks and remove the meat from the bone.
5. Discard the bone and stir the ham back into the beans. Cook for an additional 15 minutes

Talkin' 'bout beer, Growlers have made a comeback. In the late 1800s, early 1900s, you could get a pail of beer from the saloon to carry home. Some say the name came from the sound the beer made as it sloshed around, others think it's from the "growling" noise the pail made when it was pushed across the bar.

And if you want a beer to drink with your beans, you would order a John Barleycorn or a Purge or, of course, a Hop Juice.

Refried Mexican Strawberry Beans

Onions and garlic most likely would not have been used in the original recipe but they make this dish so much more flavorsome I went ahead and added them.

Mexican Strawberry beans is one of the things red beans would have been called. If you'd rather, you can make these with pinto beans.

- 2 cups red beans
- 2 tbsp lard or bacon fat
- 6 cups water (to cover beans plus 2 inches)
- 1 tsp salt
- 2 tsp pepper (or to taste)
- 1/2 cup chopped onion
- 1 clove garlic, minced (optional)

1. Rinse pinto beans thoroughly with cold water
2. Cook onions in the lard or bacon fat 'til soft
3. Transfer beans, onions, salt and pepper and garlic, if using, into slow cooker
4. Add enough water to 2 inches above beans.
5. Cook on HIGH for 6 - 8 hours or until most of the water has been soaked up
6. Use a masher to mash to a refried consistency. Serve warm

COWBOY CROCK POT COOKING: OTHER VITTLES

Chuck Wagon Buffalo Stew

Buffalo is much leaner than other meats, which can make it tough but with slow crock pot cooking it will melt in your mouth.

It used to be said the best way to cook this was to throw it in a pot with a horseshoe. When the horseshoe got soft and tender, you could eat the meat.

- 1 lb buffalo stewing meat and ½ lb rabbit, cut in cubes
- OR 1 ½ lb. buffalo meat ('cause some people don't like hare in their food)
- 12 small potatoes, cubed
- ½ cup chopped onions
- 8-oz. carrots, diced
- 16-oz can diced tomatoes
- 2 cups beef broth
- ½ cup flour
- 1 tablespoon Worcestershire sauce
- 1 tablespoon honey
- 1 teaspoon dried marjoram leaves
- Salt and pepper to taste
- 12 oz beer

1. Dredge meat in the flour then combine with all other ingredients in the crock pot
2. Cover and turn on high for one hour then reduce to low for 6 hours, or cook on low for at least 8 hours

By the 1880s, between white hunters and American Indians not more than a few thousand buffalo (more properly called Bison) were left alive to roam. These days, the herds have grown back, and bison meat is readily available online if you can't find it in a local store.

Potato and Onion Soup

I know… this has bacon *and* butter. If that scares you, go ahead and leave out the butter, but it's so much richer with it in.

And if you didn't know it, onions were sometimes referred to as skunk eggs. Bacon might be called overland trout or sowbelly. The term "overland trout" was first printed in 1887 but for the life of me, I can't figure where it came from.

- ½ lb bacon
- 4 cups cubed peeled potatoes
- 4 cups chicken stock
- 2 cups finely chopped onions
- 1/4 cup cow grease (that's another term for butter)
- 1/4 tsp. ground black pepper

- 1 qt milk
- Salt and pepper

1. Fry the bacon, remove from the pan and chop
2. Drain half the fat from the pan and saute the onion
   lightly
3. Add all the ingredients except the milk to the crock pot
4. Cover and cook on low for 7 – 8 hours
5. Add the milk, stir well and continue to heat for 20 – 30
   minutes

Hash Brown Casserole

This makes enough for a small posse of cowboys.

- 1 (30-ounce) package of plain frozen hash brown potatoes
- 12 whole eggs
- 1 cup milk
- 12 oz diced ham
- 1/2 onion, chopped
- 1 1/2 cups shredded cheddar cheese
- ½ tsp dried sage
- 1 tsp each of salt and pepper

1. Grease the inside of your crock
2. Break up the hash browns and spread them on the bottom
3. In a large bowl, whisk together the eggs, milk, sage, salt and pepper
4. Stir in the ham, onion, and cheese
5. Pour this mixture evenly over the hash browns
6. Cover and cook on low for 6 to 8 hours, or on high for 3 to 4 hours. The edges should be nicely browned

Rattlesnake Stew

Tastes like chicken? Nah. Not really. Rattlesnake has a more gamey taste but, cooked right, you'll appreciate its unique flavor. Oh, and if you're not going to go out and shoot yourself a rattler you can find the meat online, but it will cost you big time.

- 2 pounds of rattlesnake meat
- 1 onion chopped
- 1 cup of chopped celery
- 4 medium potatoes diced
- 1 tablespoon of minced garlic
- 1 cup of chopped carrots
- 15 ounce can of diced tomatoes
- salt and pepper to taste
- 1 tsp ketchup

- 1 tsp steak sauce
- 1 14 ounce can of beef broth
- 2 tablespoons of cornstarch
- Pinch of sugar
- ¼ cup of lemon juice

1. Simmer rattlesnake meat in water and lemon juice for 1 hr
2. Remove and separate the meat from the bones
3. Mix meat with the rest of the ingredients in the crock pot
4. Cover and cook on low for 8 hours

Deer Pot Roast

Eating well was sometimes a question of opportunity. If you had a chance to bag a deer or other game, you took it.

- 3 - 4 lb venison roast
- 2 or 3 tbsp plain flour
- Salt and pepper
- 2 tbsp lard or oil
- ½ cup chopped onion
- 2 cloves minced garlic
- 1 tsp dry mustard
- 1 cup beef broth
- 1 cup red wine
- 1 cup red currant jelly

1. Sprinkle roast with salt and pepper; dust with flour
2. Brown the venison in heated oil or lard
3. Remove the meat and add the onion to skillet; saute 'til just beginning to turn brown
4. Add beef broth and red currant jelly; warm, without boiling, 'til the jelly dissolves and scrape any browned bits from the bottom of the pan
5. Transfer to crock pot with the roast, garlic, mustard and wine
6. Cover and cook on LOW for 9 to 12 hours, until pot roast is tender

Calf's Head Soup

OK, the original c1900 recipe calls for you to "remove the brains from the calf's head. Put the head in 4 quarts of cold water and cook till meat drops from the bone-3 or 4 hours…….. Season the brains with salt and pepper and butter and beat together with 1 raw egg."

I reckon most of you won't want to do that (even if you could get a calf's head these days), so I'm going with beef shanks and good old sausage balls.

Another recipe from 1879 includes carrots (but I've omitted them here) and suggests browning a little sugar in a pan (caramelizing) and mixing with wine before adding to the soup.

- 2 lbs beef shank (you could also use pork ribs or chicken thighs, or a mix of all three)
- 3 onions, chopped fine
- 6 cloves
- 1 cup ketchup or wine (seriously, that's the original 1900 recipe)
- ½ lb sausage meat
- 2 eggs
- Dry crackers, pounded to dust
- Salt and pepper
- 2 lemons, sliced thin

1. Put the shank in the crock pot and cover with water

2. Add the onion and cloves, cover and cook for at least 6 hours on low

3. Remove the shanks and take the meat off them. Cut up the meat and return it to the broth with the cup of ketchup or wine

4. Stir and let cook another 30 minutes while you prepare the sausage balls

5. Mix 1 beaten egg with the sausage meat and salt and pepper

6. Make the sausage into balls, roll in the other beaten egg and cracker dust

7. Fry the balls a rich brown then drop them in the soup with the lemon slices and serve immediately

Mouse Pie

I couldn't resist this one. And, hey! If you're a hungry cowboy on the trail, any vittles taste good.

- 5 fat field mice
- 1 cup macaroni
- 1/2 thinly sliced medium onion
- 16 oz can tomatoes
- 1 – 2 cups water
- Salt and pepper

1. Fry the field mice long enough to rend out some of the excess fat
2. Grease a crock pot with some of this fat and put a layer of macaroni in it
3. Add field mice and cover with remaining macaroni
4. Add onions and seasoning, then tomatoes and enough water to fill the crock about 1 inch above the macaroni
5. Cover and cook on high for 1 hour. Check. If needed, lower heat and cook another 20 – 30 minutes 'til the mice are well done

I'm thinkin' some of you aren't quite ready for mice yet, so you go on and substitute a few sausages instead.

COWBOY CROCK POT COOKING: SWEET STUFF

Spotted Pup

After the Civil War, rice farming moved from the east to Arkansas, Louisiana and Texas. Spotted Pup is the name cowpokes gave to raisins cooked in rice.

Most folk like to top the pudding with whipped cream. In my family, we used gin. (Just sayin')

- 3/4 cup long-grain white rice
- 1 cup raisins

- 3 cups milk
- 3/4 cup granulated sugar
- 1 pinch salt
- 1/3 cup butter, melted

1. Put all the ingredients in a lightly buttered crock pot and stir
2. Cover and cook on HIGH for 2 1/2 to 3 hours, until rice has absorbed the liquid. Check after about an 1 ½ hours to give a stir and see if you might need to add a little more milk

Cowboy Crock Pot Apple Pie

- 8 tart apples, peeled and sliced
- ½ cup nuts, broken up
- 1 1/4 teaspoons ground cinnamon
- 1 1/4 teaspoon nutmeg
- 3/4 cup milk
- 2 tablespoons butter, softened
- 3/4 cup brown sugar
- 2 eggs
- 1 teaspoon vanilla
- 1/2 cup Bisquick mix
- 1 cup Bisquick mix
- 1/3 cup brown sugar
- 3 tablespoons cold butter

1. Lightly grease the crock
2. In a large bowl, toss the apples and walnuts with the cinnamon and nutmeg and place in the crock pot
3. In another bowl, whisk together the milk, softened butter, ¾ cup sugar, eggs, vanilla and the 1/2 cup Bisquick. Spoon over the apples
4. In another bowl, combine 1 cup Bisquick with 1/3 cup sugar. With a knife cut the cold butter into the mixture then rub between your fingers 'til it resembles bread crumbs. Sprinkle this mixture over the top of the apple mixture
5. Cover and cook on low 6 - 7 hours. The crumb topping should be a golden brown

Indian Pudding

Here's a much-simplified version of another turn-of-the-century recipe. The original called for half a pint of New Orleans molasses, which I believe is unsulphured molasses. At any rate, that's what we're using here.

- 2 cups yellow cornmeal
- 1 pint unsulphured molasses
- ½ c. butter
- ½ tsp. salt
- ½ tsp. soda
- 4 eggs
- 3 qts hot milk

1. Mix all of the ingredients with half of the milk in a saucepan
2. Stirring constantly, bring to a simmer
3. Remove from the heat and stir in the rest of the milk
4. Transfer to a crock pot and cook on low for 6 – 8 hours
5. Best way to serve this is with vanilla ice cream

Brent Younger is the:

BRENT YOUNGER

I love to cook. And I love to eat. Over the years I've collected and created thousands of recipes. These aren't eat-yourself-thin kind of recipes. Don't get me wrong. I like lettuce. But I'm a hard-working stiff, probably like you, and at the end of the day I want something I can really wrap my appetite around. Not that I don't use quality ingredients. In fact, that's critical to good food. I grew up with a dad who was an avid gardener so I know all about fresh. And Mom was a great cook. Money was pretty scarce but Mom could make a feast out of a bit of meat and a bunch of Dad's veggies – you'd think you were eating ambrosia.

Anyway, I figured it was time I started sharing some of my recipes. Most of them are pretty inexpensive and pretty easy to put together.

You might just be wondering if I've ever made the Mouse Pie. Well, I'm not saying. Why don't you try it yourself and let me know what you think?

I hope you enjoyed this book and will consider giving it a favorable review. Independent authors have a tough time competing with the big guys and we rely heavily on you, the reader, for your feedback and to spread the word about books you enjoy. Thanks!

And join me on facebook where you'll find new recipes from time to time:

www.facebook.com/truckstopgourmet

Brent Younger

13402956R00048